6+5 Poetry

Maryam Atcha

BookLeaf Publishing

India | USA | UK

Presentation by *BookLeaf Publishing*

Web: www.bookleafpub.com

E-mail: info@bookleafpub.com

ISBN: 9789395756532

First edition 2022

DEDICATION

To the One Most High. All Praise is due only to
You.

PREFACE

From childhood, I always sought true, untainted love above all endevours. This however, proved to be an arduous and painful journey in a material reductionist world. Poetry became a means of creative, written self-expression when I felt the most stifled and silenced. Through writing and reading poetry, I was able to heal from many heartbreaks. I hope by sharing my works with you, the reader, you too may find solace in my art.

Young one

I loved my mommy first
I loved my daddy too
Who knew that not long after, I would forget
how to love me through and through

I searched for love in places it would not, could
not be
I put my trust in boxes and internalised that no
one would genuinely help me

And so it followed, I would lose my way and
lose that much more time

But Guide-He never abandoned me
And "One Day" did come
And so,

I forgave my mommy first
I forgave my daddy too
Who knew that not long after I would learn to
forgive me through and through

For my first

Mini-me, sweet pea
Nothing can stop your rising
Take the world by storm

For my son

Strong and sweet, at peace
Funny and cute-Little Moose
Full of love and hugs

Dams

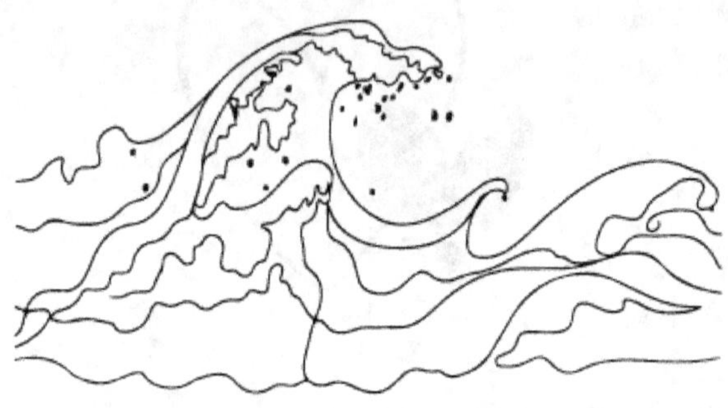

Remove your dams
Remove your barriers and break down your
walls
Open up all channels
Leave not a single one barred and let the river of
my love
Flow through to you
These pure waters seek you.
Because don't you know?
Life begets life.
The source of this love is True and Eternal
So lose not hope. Nor faith
Let the blessings and beauty run their unbridled
course
Straight to you
Straight through to your heart

To the darkest parts left abandoned and yearning
for new life for
So long
Will you stop the gardens from growth?
Have courage in the darkness beloved
And let my love in....

Oh Love

Oh Love, you have me in a dream state while awake

My body remains earthbound, while my spirit soars above

In your presence

7

In your presence, my past, present and future all merge into one

At the close

I hope to find you again. At the end of all things.

Mirror

I love all the parts of you that are in me, and I
love all the parts of me that are in you, and I
love all the parts of you that are just you, and I
love all the parts of me that are just me

Compass

Oh lovers, always follow your heart for it shall
not lead you astray

Twin flame

11

Look at you beautiful King, embracing your
Divine Feminine and Masculine

The abyss

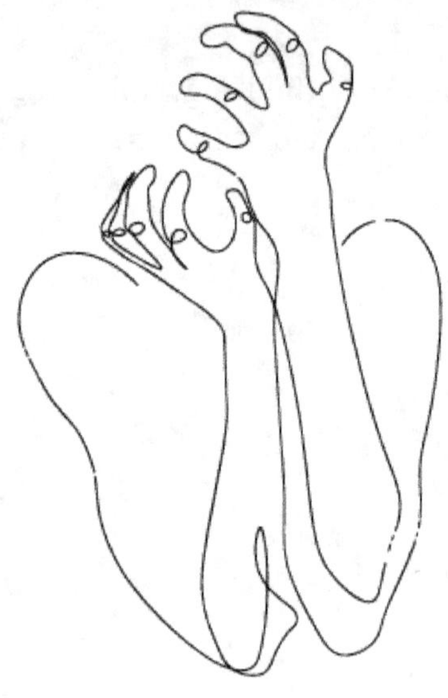

If my sadness within were to crack and break through the barricades of this resilient heart, then it would flood everything in its surroundings without feeling or care. The undulating waves of despair would swallow up all neighbouring houses and streets. All the vibrant colours would be smeared and marred with melancholic grief.

Teacher

A heart so pure that it reflected the Divine. The only separation between him and God was a single veil. He bore our salvation and serenity so graciously. May Blessings and Peace continue to flow wherever his memory goes

Soul song

Oh my cherished one, I know
I know there were eons
I know there were ages
I know there were lifetimes
In this separation
I know there were years and months
I know there were weeks and days
I know there were minutes and seconds that
My heart sang this song
Sang this song just for you

Only you

15

Beloved King, our heart and spirit are two rivers
leading to the same sea.
Your soul finds its twin within me

Reconcile

How could I possibly have meant nothing to you
and you everything to me?
My world, post you, was left completely anew
Perhaps the nothing was in you and the
everything was in me?
Your spirit just reflecting all my love back to
me.
Silently,
Indifferently,
Reflecting all that was beautiful, whole and
vibing high in me
I feel no ways about it now.
No resentment.
No bitterness.
I leave now- the past of you-
With gratitude.
And grace.
As I continue this path, this journey,
Alone.
And save face

Best friend

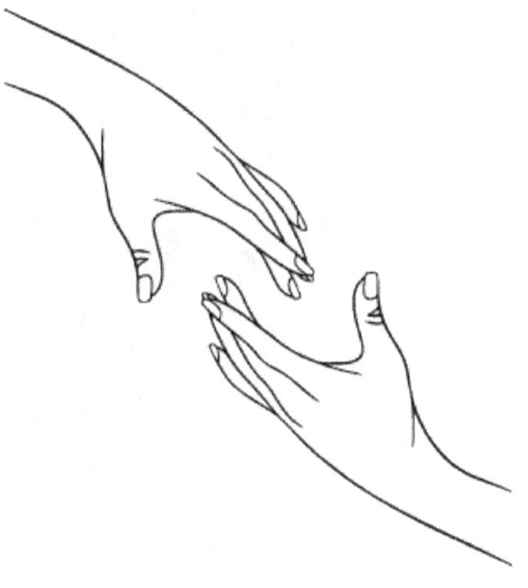

Arrived right on time
Beautiful, as can be,
Her presence brings peace

In this moment

I am in this moment
Perfectly still
No grief and no weak need, overtakes me
I am in this moment
Perfectly whole
I need no saviour without me
For she has always been within me
Suitors and lovers approach me
Some filled with wanton, brutal lust
Yet
I am in this moment
Free of all sloppy need
I am in this moment
Free to *dream*
Free to breathe
Free to heal
Free to speak
Free to BE
I am in this moment
Authentically me.

Prince Charming?

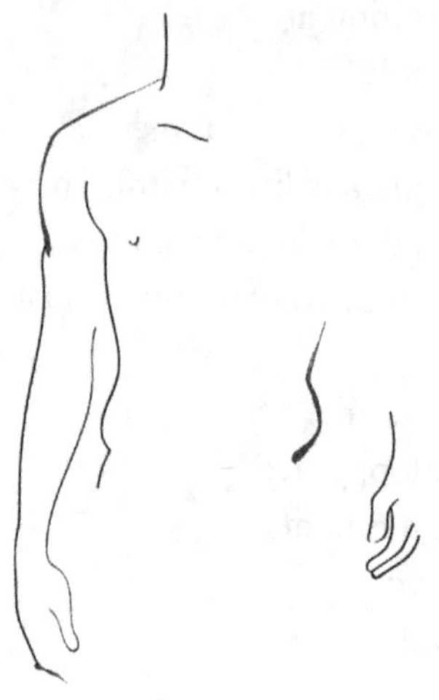

With his light brown hair and those blue eyes
inviting me
Awakening me
to new possibilities
Baby girl no more fears, only ease
Is he everything he seems to be?
Coming in with these new frequencies
What could it all mean for me?
Permeated something in my psyche
Even for a moment in time
I don't ask for forever. Not anymore
I just need to be free of these binds

On tears and weeping shut the door
Baby boy, will this be destinies entwined?
Only one way to find out. Only one way to see
I have to leave it all behind. Spread wings and
fly free.

What lies ahead

From among the ruins of my shattered past,
Two roads emerge
Both beckoning me to my destiny
But from one path I must diverge
Both are getting the best of me
Opposing possibilities
Two lovers in my fantasies
One with his clear blue eyes and perfectly
coiffed hair, no need for tears, just ease and
genuine care
But the other with his caramel skin and soulful
eyes
To him, all my love laid painfully bare

Which road to take and which path to choose?

A Soul Twin or a Fairytale King
I am not ready to risk all, not ready to lose

Perhaps, for now, I will just choose me, Choose
peace.
Lovely and sweet.
And perhaps in this way, will the way be
prepared for me

Unrequited ove

I loved and loved and loved
I gave and gave and gave
Without knowing me
Without knowing you
Uncommitted men
Selfish men
Narcissistic and damaged men
Men who were too busy or who cared too little
Men who had no intentions long-term with me
Liars and thieves got the best of me
I loved them for all the things missing inside of
me
Or rather, all the things I believed I could never
be:
Strong
And whole
And fearless
Not knowing I had to step into my power
Step back into me
Not knowing, not until now,
That the search for love began
by searching, for it all, within me
Not knowing, not until now, that all that faculty I
gave away, should have all been poured back
into me

His smile

I remember our paths crossing once or twice
But
The years had since passed between us
I never thought of him until now
Recently
Our paths have crossed again
More frequently.
The focus and intent in his light eyes
When they come to rest on my face
The way he looks at me
Differently
In a way, I have never seen
Is he asking the same questions as me?
Also, wondering about all our possibilities?
Yesterday,
He smiled at me
The curve in his lips changing the look that
usually rests upon his exquisite face
That smile told me he was suppressing his real
desire and feelings for me
Desires and feelings I know all too well because
the same feelings, for him, reside in me

Fantasy

Let me be the Aphrodite to your Adonis
The Cinderella to your Charming
The Jasmine to your Aladdin

Avert not your eyes from my gaze
Hold me in your strong arms
Built to keep out the storms
I will fill your spirit with peace
And love

The promise of tomorrow wanes
But we have today
And that is all you and I need
To fulfill our destiny

Let me show you a way unknown
To your reality
Because I am not of this world
I belong to the Unseen
And here, with me, will you find complete
All your dreams

Intoxication

I don't touch any drink, but your ocean eyes
have me inebriated
I know you want a taste of my red wine
I will also leave you intoxicated
You won't touch any other drink, after me
Built like an Adonis
Hold me like velvet Venus
Like you, I don't play any games
But it does not mean I don't love your pursuit
This dance of desire
Inspired movement and joy
The secret smiles of long time admirers
Come a little closer
And let us set fire to everything in our way

I'll be good

I won't drain your pockets
Won't harm your heart
Won't make you cry

I will carry your seed
Will keep the faith
Will give my all

Loving you is easy
Loving you is like breathing

I will be that woman if you are that man

Destinies Entwined

You are falling in love in this distance
I know this, so this is the only reason I await you
with patience.
Words, between us, can be far and few but our
beating hearts are witness!
We meet in the flesh and in dream states too
My eyes they speak this language of love and
desire for you
Your eyes, mirror mine, and also spill their
secrets and truth
We can hide and mask, behind circumstances

But our bodies are baring full proof.
Divine
Alignment-
Won't allow prolonged confinement-
With flying colours we will fulfill our destined
assignment.

Is this love?

I am starting to count the hours and the days
My heart-for you- is relentless
Waiting for those fleeting moments of happiness
Sweet bliss
For us to be in close distances
Sweet glimpses
To know you are good
To know you still want my company and
Time-
I give it freely to you as I should
You know I would
Ask me for anything and I could
Remember? I promised I'll be good
I promise I will try
And if not now then for sure
In Time

Three plus Six

I wished to write a single poem for you but one
turned to eleven
In this short period
Perhaps it is the muse in you and the poet in me-
Connecting
Imagine if we chose one another?
Chose alignment and compatibility-
Imagine all the possibilities.
I would take inspiration like Neruda or
Browning or The Bard.
I would fill pages and pages with poetry.
Because love only knows its own quality. Free
of vanity, it only seeks its own reflection
I have nothing to lose and everything to gain
No more questioning.
And you also know who you are to me
So go ahead King
and risk it all,
Let us take this leap of faith
with this once in a lifetime
Chance.

Raj

Last night I dreamt of you again
We locked eyes for a moment
My insecurities and fears
You stripped them with ease
Your bright eyes, sincere and true
Told me I was everything you value
They told me you would never bring me harm
That you would never lie to me or betray your
appointed charge
Your majestic beauty in my dreams also reflects
in our reality
A single look did everything needed to give my
anxious spirit peace

Ego death

I was sixteen; young and naive
And seeking fairytale love.
In my innocence I believed Arqam was my one.
Oh how first heartbreak so bitterly stung.
So I tried to make Mario what he was not;
Attempted for too long to fit circle into square.
I wasted my early twenties believing I had time
to spend and spare.
Shad left me shattered and
Stefan left me battered
With Josh I grieved for years, convinced my
flame twin was it, tried so hard to bridge the
silences and rifts.
yet here I remain, as if born anew,
I venture on. For love is weaved into my genetic
makeup and soul essence.
This is the state in which I fell for you.
So go ahead, let them gossip, let them question-
both my integrity and moral compass
I am no longer afraid or scared to lose
All I want is to remain here in this moment
Happy, peaceful, joyful, present.

Soul contract

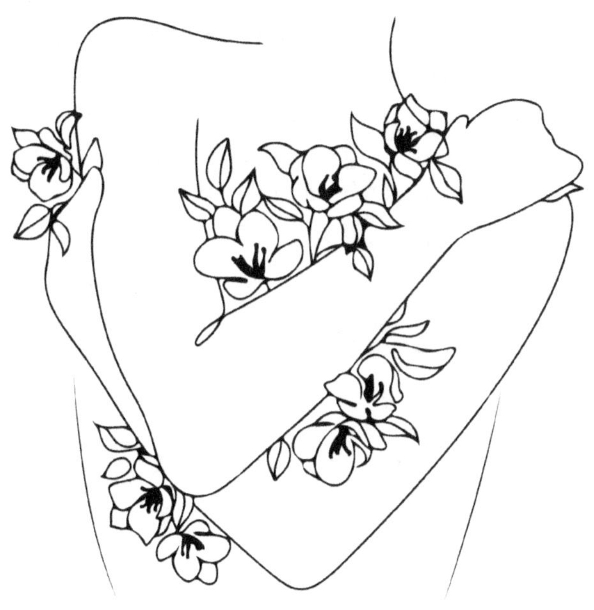

Perhaps I made a soul contract with Creator
before I came
Here on this earthly plane
To experience His Love in every kind of way
But the exception was it would come with every
kind of pain
And this is why I am asked to patiently remain
I cannot look ahead at my future now with
disdain

For I am not done with love and have yet much
to gain
In the past I knew too many narcissists and even
a twin flame
But soulmate love I have yet to fully attain
And for this adventure and next steps my target
is clear and my arrow is fully aimed

Six plus Five

Truly I love everybody, all of humanity.
But falling in love, it can't be with just anybody
It really takes a very special somebody
Whose spirit reflects the inner me
So when I do fall, it happens so easily-
Flawlessly.

And if the conditions permit I will remain in that
state for eternity
As long as there is genuine reciprocity, Divine
connection and matching energy,
I devote myself entirely
So readily
Offering
A love completely free
of ego, pride and apathy